Twin – Flame Truths

Registered ® June 2019 by Dr. Angela Heppner
ISBN: 9781099260162

I0420722

Copyright 2019 – Dr. Angela Heppner

Contact: Heppner@gmx.com

About The Author

Dr. Angela Heppner owns advanced degrees in divinity – holistic medicine, marriage counseling and relationships. She walks, writes, loves and lives according to the teachings, experiences and degrees that are in her possession. Dr. Heppner has written this book to share her knowledge and truths with all of mankind in hopes to sort out the mass confusion blanketing the globe in the seemingly mad dash of one and all to reunite with their own Twin – Flame.

Accolades

There comes a time in ones life when you stop chasing empty promises and exhibiting foolish behavior. It is then when you realize that you need the truth in order to find that one true person who will light up your life like a Christmas tree. The truth that is found is completely contained in this wonderful book and the madness that once consumed my life is no more. Everything I ever needed to know about Twin – Flames is presented here and there is nothing confusing or contradictory about it. I'm so happy to have straightened out my relationship disasters through this book and find myself pointing in the right direction.

Elizabeth Prentiss

Fascinating! I had no idea that there were so many different ways that one could get side tracked in their search for their Twin – Flame. It's just ridiculous how desperate some people make themselves and follow all of these bizarre methods that don't ever make sense. I have to say that I'm glad I skipped over all of those misguiding notions described in this book and allowed the truth that Dr. Heppner writes to guide me successfully. It's a small price to pay to relieve yourself from the heartache and disillusion that will come if you blindly follow everything that comes your way regarding Twin – Flames. I absolutely recommend this book to anyone who has even the slightest desire to seek out their true Twin – Flame. Dr. Heppner has done such a wonderful job in presenting this topic in a truthful and straight forward manner.

Anne Marie Collins

In an age where you are hit from every angle by falsehoods and greed mongers, it is such a relief to read a book filled with true passion and desire to spread the truth. I came across this book on a recommendation from a friend and could not control my excitement as I read it. It's brilliant lay out and easy to read language leaves no room for doubts about whether or not you will understand it or not. I am quite obsessed with finding my

Twin – Flame and after searching high and low for something useful; it's quite a refreshing change to read something that does not try to trick me into some awful methodology which will never work anyhow. It's a wonderful thing to be more confident about what your needs are on this topic and I am so excited to have found the way to liberate myself from everything but the truth about Twin – Flames

Agnes Montoya

Wow, what a beautiful book cover but is it certainly not the best part to say the least. I was absolutely fascinated and amazed at all of the wonderful information in this book and it all made so much sense to me, I still cannot get over how much garbage there is circulating these days about Twin-Flames and I am glad that Dr Heppner has set the record straight. I am so in love with this book and it has immediately become my Twin-Flame bible.

Anne Marie Raspussen

What more can I say? This book was an incredible eye-opener for me and at times made me embarrassed to realize how many foolish mistakes I've made in trying to find my Twin-Flame. There was a time when I believed all of the myths about Twin-Flames that Dr. Heppner so clearly and completely disputes and I am finally on the right path to where I wish to be. I know now that as a result of reading this book and following its guidance, I have the best chances of reuniting with my Twin-Flame.

Ellie McKenna

Acknowledgements

I cannot help but be so incredibly thankful and grateful for all the Divine assistance I've had in writing this book. Certainly my life experiences and research have played a big part in being able to formulate this text; but it was the encouragement and guidance from above that made this dream a reality. Over the course of several years I had gone from one relationship to another like many others seeking out my True Twin – Flame and yet something; often several things; were always missing. I must say that it is from those experiences that I've learned a great many things about what a True Spiritual Connection should be.

I am grateful that I had to kiss a number of frogs to get to a Prince because it showed me how worthwhile true life experiences can be and I write about them in this book. I hope that by reading this book – you will be well prepared to meet your twin-flame. It is the journey of a lifetime for many and one which must not be taken lightly; nor rushed in anyway as you will see it is a precise process that must be adhered to in order to be successful.

Many thanks to you for taking the time to read about this passion of mine and I am quite certain you will feel just how much heart I have put into it.

Twin – Flame Truths
by Dr. Angela Heppner

Contents

_____

Welcome

The light will show you the way if you let it. Find your way through all of the fallacies and misleading banter as you search for the truth regarding Twin – Flame Connections. See how one can be deceived by the typical signs that many share which would lead you to believe that you have found your Twin – Flame. There's so much written on this topic, that it would be a miracle if you were not utterly confused. See for yourself through factual details and Dr. Heppner's real life experiences how it can be an incredible challenge and an occasional nightmare to wade through all of the concepts out there right now.

Do yourself a favor before you make another move in the wrong direction and let your heart and mind be open to these wonderful words of wisdom shared in this book. You will explore the fascinating world of True Spiritual Connections and in return be able to cast aside those things that you will see make no sense at all. It is Gods will when two Twins come together and it is only through his guidance that they remain that way. So come along and delight in this joyous expression of True – Love written from a first – hand point of view.

Chapter One

Introduction

The Twin - Flame Connection is a sacred and unique gift that symbolizes ones devotion and adherence to the love and mercy of God. It is only when the two are following the Christ Conscious Path completely that this amazing gift from God is bestowed upon them. They were made by God in the beginning as souls in Heaven or elsewhere and by a sheer miracle meet on the earth to share in a relationship. There is no way around this - one cannot merely hope and pray that their Twin - Flame will show up on their door step, try to manifest them or draw them forward through some means of energy or otherwise practices; this is something that must be earned to receive and one must also continue to earn it through their life.

A Twin - Flame Connection is not delivered to you on a silver platter; you cannot expect that everything will be initially perfect and flawless. There will be some adjustments that need to be made usually one or the other will have challenges and need to sort things out in order to reach the level of the other. There is much work involved in reuniting even though the spark between the two has never died. You should expect a period of adjustment and re-acquaintance as the two energies familiarize themselves with each other again. Take the time to evaluate the needs and desires of both halves and you will find that together they properly compliment each other in a most Divine way. Prepare yourself for what might be ahead as it is a continuation of the process of earning this special and sacred re-connection.

Make magic and inspire yourself from these things you create. Hold hands with your mate as you walk down the Christ Conscious Path and see what it truly means to be alive and in the light of Gods love. You cannot claim to know or have met your Twin – Flame if you do not know yourself and have the proper relationship with God

You cannot avoid this requirement; nor circumvent that which draws you in because it is the spirit of life and love that generates and warrants your connection with the one true body and spirit that matches your own. It is all in Gods hands and He has the final say; but beyond that, you alone have the ability to earn the blessed and Divine gift of being re-connected with your Twin – Flame by living, practicing and fully becoming a part of the Christ Conscious Path.

Chapter Two

The Basics

There are seven vital components and musts that make up a true Twin – Flame connection. If these are not present or a part of this Divinely blessed connection it is not a Twin – Flame connection; nor is it genuine.

1. Christ Conscious path for both
2. The Moon
3. The Eyes
4. Past Lives
5. Physical Similarities
6. Enchanted Spirits
7. Tantric Energy Connection

Without the Christ Conscious path there is no reason for the two to be connected and this gift will not be presented to them. They will just be two ships passing in the night.

The moon represents light and purity and a strong physical connection. It is not out of the ordinary and in fact a facet of this Divine connection for the two to have uncanny skills regarding the moon such as viewing and see it in exactly the same fashion. They are apt to see the same faces, structures and even more than one moon side by side. There is a familiarity in the eyes between the two; but more than that.
In those eyes you can see into the past of what you had. What was gained and lost; but you also must be ready to see it and open to it or it to will pass you by.

The two will always share or would have shared many past lives together. Those who are spiritually open and attuned will be fully open to and aware of this. They will either have visions, dreams or visit their pasts together via meditation.

There are also many physical uncanny similarities between the two. The nose, the hands, feet and the eyes. There are many physical attributes that would indicate this connection. The two also have enriched enchanted spirits. When both are truly themselves; they are identical. In some cases; both wild, free, playful – conjoined in the most intimate of details. Like looking into the mirror and seeing the same personality look right back at them.

The Tantric energy connection of the Twin – Souls is out of this world. Upon meeting the energies and sexual experiences are bar none. As time goes on, their bodies become more in tune with one another. The energetic connection is on fire and their fluids, movements and excitement become identical. It can also even get to the point where the two climax at exactly the same time without any effort or thought. This is what a true Twin – Flame connection is. The heat they feel and continue to feel exemplifies that; it's the arousing connective nature when Twin – Souls unite and collide. What you must remember is that your souls were once one and now they are remembering what each other likes and what will please them best on a more subconscious level.

This is why you are not always aware; but doing things differently perhaps because it's not always in the motions or actions; but rather in the way that your energies work together. In this type of connection, these things soon become automatic without the intervention of the human aspect. It's one of Gods great gifts to you – to experience this. This is also quite rare and almost must be earned between the couple; just as a true Twin – Flame couple are only those who walk, live and practice the Christ Conscious path teachings and principals. Often the point in their paths are different; but complimentary and if you add them up between them, they are complete and balance out. What one is lacking, the other can provide and so forth.

They have a metaphysical connection above anything physical or emotional. They can connect in unexplainable ways that do not need an explanation – for their spirits and souls are forever joined as one. Lastly, they are much the same age and have many similar past lives – age meaning soul– spiritual age. More often than not, they will have had several lives together; but also many apart. They may not have successfully connected in the past in the way they had hoped for; but they were together and they have been searching and seeking each other over time. They will know in an instant when they have found their true love.

They have complimentary wings – each with one wing to fully fly. It does not mean that they cannot fly without the other; but rather to have the best flight experience they need both. This is true on a relationship level and of course when they combine all that the glory and of

God and all the gifts he has given them – those two together cannot do anything but succeed.

It is their reward you might say accepting, embracing, serving God and accepting his love to follow the Christ Conscious path. It is truly all about love and not just the love between the two of them; but the love they give to others and how they present themselves along the way. This is the only way that you will have your Twin – Flame connection.

Any other way by any other means is not a Twin – Flame connection; but instead a fallacy, connection and trick to keep you away from your true Twin – Flame; for Satan does not want you to be connected because it is so beautiful, holy and divine. It is the way, the truth and the light. And very few people have this very special gift. It is truly an honor to be connected like that and you will know when yours comes along – you will feel it and you will not be able to turn away.

In the next few chapters I am going to take you on a journey of discovery into further detail and exploration of some very key essentials, truths and genuine Twin – Flame components. Welcome to Gods perfection!

Chapter Three

The Higher – Self

Your heart knows many things; but there are a few instances where you will need a bit more confirmation – especially when it comes to knowing your True Twin – Flame. There will be times when several things line up between the two of you; but even that sort of connection is not enough. This is where your higher – self comes in. It is a knowing, a full fledged confirmation from the highest possible source within you.

But how do you know that the voice you hear is actually your higher – self? It comes down to this; you have a rash, not only of deep penetrating feelings of peace and adornment; but also there is this essential pull that for lack of better terms smacks you in the face. It can be said that it is nothing like you've ever experienced before. But wait, you might say I've been having many new feelings as of late regarding this person.

So how do I identify that one particular and unique presence? Well, in fact that's the key – it is accompanied by an awareness that a very strong presence is surrounding you. You cannot see it – nor understand it; but by its mere existence, you will get the message that this is the one. You may hear their name screamed within your ear; or get a warm feeling and thought about this person that will accompany this presence.

It will be like the most peaceful earth quake you can imagine and yet, it may almost knock you off your feet.

That is certainly a contradiction of course; but it is meant to send you a strong message and yet give you peace about it as well. By in large, you will not see it coming, you may be out at the store taking care of business; or even sitting at your table having dinner. It is truly not something that anyone else will notice; but when you get this, it will seem like the earth is shaking.

At first you will probably not understand it as it will come so unexpectedly; but after a short while, you will realize what it means. Again, it is part of the knowing that every human has; but that very few generally experience. This is how I can best explain it and so your experience may be slightly different. In the end, the message will be delivered loud and clear and will be your only way in confirming that you have truly met your Twin – Flame.

Chapter Four

Christ Conscious Path

It is a simple concept to put into words; but not so simple to put into action. Taking up your cross each day and carrying it with you through thick and thin and both easy and hard times can be quite the challenge. But what does it truly mean to take up your cross? It certainly does not mean to carry the weight of the world on your shoulders as perhaps Jesus has done. What it means is to live each day in harmony with yourself and the love that God gives unto you and holding that tightly within your heart.

Furthermore, it means to share all that love with others despite their actions, words or feelings towards you. That is where the cross comes in and represents the weight of a negative and thoughtless behavior from others that will burden you and provide quite the challenge in your attempts to keep going along the straight and narrow. It requires much strength and courage to both carry a cross in a physical sense as well as in a metaphorical sense.

Yet the load can be the same and in this sense that I speak of, it will come from every angle and you may end up with what seems like multiple crosses. Now, to stay on the Christ Conscious Path, you cannot throw off your cross at the first bump in the road; but you will actually have to hold on tighter and stay firm in your beliefs. This is where our greatest challenge lies; to keep a living and open heart even when it seems that you are the only one doing so.

In the past it may have been easy, for you may have not been this pure and aware as you are now; but as you go further along the path of perfection, it becomes quite a challenge to not let others interfere in your service of God. It is a matter of spreading kind words and deeds even in the most horrendous of situations and especially on days when you are feeling down and out or perhaps even grouchy. They say that there is no rest for the weary and that is also true for those on the Christ Conscious Path.

You must often ask yourself what would Jesus do in this situation? Especially if you have your doubts about the best way in which to handle it; but even more basic than that, is to know that if a thought or words or actions are not coming from your heart – then it is truly not something that Jesus would do. You must over – look many things that others may send your way; but that also does not mean that you should be a punching bag.

Separate yourself from people in situations that are not loving and kind and then send your love from afar. Even on the Christ Conscious Path, you have the right to protect yourself and need not throw yourself into the middle of a war zone as that is not bright at all. It is only when you are in situations that you can't avoid, where you must do your best to shine brightly. A lot of work?

Absolutely; but it is the only way to reach full awareness of yourself and others and the love that can be present in all of us. At the same time, it is an absolute prerequisite to finding and retaining your True

Twin – Flame. Anything else is a fallacy and will lead you down a path of despair, disappointment and illusions that will lead you everywhere but where you want to be.

Chapter Five

Spiritual Gifts

It's wonderful when two people connect in a Divine and Spiritual way. You then find that suddenly you have common experiences that are otherwise unexplainable. You may try to rationalize and make sense of these things; but there is no need as the gifts you may often get from the Divine need no explanation. For example, you might just share visionary abilities with your partner and see some aspects of past lives you had together and they will often come in a crystal clear way.

They will more often than not feel incredibly familiar, even though you may not be able to remember all of the details. You will get a strong feeling in your heart to signify that what you see is in fact your past reality. This will happen more and more as time goes by and it will be much more familiar and emotional as you bring back memories that were lost so long ago. Above and beyond those experiences, you may also feel a common presence around you when you are near to each other and it will seem like a blanket which wraps you up so tightly in a loving embrace.

Each of you will have this experience; but not always at exactly the same time. The thing that you're feeling is a spiritual energy reserved for those that share this unique bond on a spiritual level. It is the Divine blessing you and keeping you close in ways that you cannot do yourself. This does not happen to others besides those who have this Twin – Flame Connection, it is yet another gift.

You may have heard of people often saying that they can finish each others sentences and things like that; but in this type of unique way, you will find that you can read not only each others mind; but also at times communicate without words above and beyond a smile, or wink or stare. It is that spiritual energy which allows this transference to occur between two halves. One does not ever need to be near the other, they might even be half a world away and it will just happen because the connection is so deep and divinely place.

Twin – Flames will also share the same sensations, for example: hot flashes, cold sweats and vibrations in their bodies that come out of nowhere which are often quite pleasant indeed. This is aside from the amazing and unfathomable sexual experiences that I speak of elsewhere in this book. I trust that by now you're realizing just how completely connected Twin – Flames are from head to toe. Bursts of energy, unexplained phenomena between the two, casual thoughts that are joined as one and a mystical, magical presence that will always surround you when they are near.

Think of that last item as an incredible and Divine hug for the love you two share so deeply. These are all rewards for your efforts and as you move further and further down the path of knowing yourselves and more importantly God, you will find that other instances unique to your own situation will present themselves as God sees fit. There are no limits to what He may bless you with as long as you remain on the Christ Conscious Path together and represent Jesus in all that you do.

Chapter Six

God

It is important that within all the things that you have your mind on that God be placed at the top of the list. It is He who gives us life and blessings and all of the beauty that surrounds us each day. Without Him, we would not exist nor experience all of these wonderful moments that come upon us if we let them and it is also He who can take them away. Your heart and your soul are products of our Divine Father and it is up to us to give thanks and be grateful each and everyday. As far as Twin – Flames are concerned, that is an even more special gift which only comes from devoting your life to serving God.

It fact, as I often mention, it is only through Him that this wonderful and Divine gift is given. Make Him the essence of your being and show the world what a remarkable gift His love can be if you allow it. Sing your songs of praise and adoration while making each moment an honorary devotion to all that He has bestowed upon you. Let nothing or nobody stand in the way of your reaching out to Him and giving glory and praise where it rightly belongs.

Many will come your way who will try to tell you that He is not so important and even that He does not exist. But that is a contradiction to the truth which is present before you each and everyday. We are put on this earth to learn many things and each situation is unique; but the common thread is that we are all to serve Him and live a life of pure and unconditional love just as He gives to us. I cannot stress enough just how important He is in your life and especially in deciding who will meet their Twin – Flame and who will not.

You may from time to time have strayed from His love; but even then He has not stopped loving you, nor turned his back on you despite what you may have done. You always have the opportunity to redeem yourself in His eyes and come back to the place where you were meant to be. It is quite vital that you keep this awareness in your heart and never think for a moment that He would give up on you. The love He has for you is unimaginable and over – whelming and it is that love which keeps you going whether you realize it or not.

Chapter Seven

Soul Matter

When I speak of souls; that does not represent anything physical or scientific; but rather that which is a non – physical entity and cannot be seen with the naked eye. It is the essence and the character and all of the loving embrace that you carry from lifetime to lifetime. It does not attach itself to your physical make up, whether we are talking about DNA or the normal energies that move through your body. It is something much more powerful and unique than any of that. The things that you feel and automatically know, meaning your intuition and so forth would work exactly the same way in any body that your soul might be placed in.

It is the underlying example of the truth about your full existence and not just about this lifetime. The body itself is just a container which allows us to exist on this plane. It could be put into a different type of creature and would still exist in the same way. When your soul was first created by God, it was so pure and light and ready for you to embark on your long journey of learning and experiences to add an interesting twist to its make up; He split it into two halves which were and still are very much identical.

You knew your other half then by way of its soul matter; the make up of this Divine entity and you were not aware, nor did it matter what body you were contained in. It is only by that knowing which may also be reinforced by past lifetimes spent together. There is no other way to know a familiar soul than through this Divine awareness.

Chapter Eight

Energy

Every human is made up of energy. Bits and pieces of matter that float around your body causing various things to occur. Our substance, brain, our heart and everything else that goes on in our everyday living is generalized by energy. But what really is energy? You could say that it is a force; a strength to allow you to move and do things; but that is not the type of energy that I am speaking about. What I mean when I mention the word energy is the Divine process of infusing your body with the Spiritual make up that you carry from lifetime to lifetime.

It retains the memory of experiences, characteristics and connections with other people, as well as the soul purpose of your existence. It floods your body throughout every vein and bone and space within it. Energy defines how you will react to certain stimuli on a physical feeling level which is not to be confused with emotional feelings. It is a vast network of sensors and reactors which light up in different colors depending upon the part of the body that you are speaking of.

There are actually seven different energy centers in the human body which are often referred to as Chakras. They are living, breathing members of your entire make up and manage the health and well – being of your non – physical self. We often do not take into consideration that when we are feeling ill or out of place that an imbalance in one of these centers could be the cause. They do require a bit of maintenance on our part in order to keep things flowing smoothly.

But how can I see what's going on with my Chakras you might ask? Well, a doctor certainly would not be able to tell you for they do not focus on or understand this higher realm of bodily function. The only way you can get in touch with and be aware of your energy centers is to become familiar with your own Spiritual – Self. People will often do meditation or yoga or a number of other things which allow you to truly get inside those workings and feel what's really going on at this higher level.

It makes sense that you would need to take a different view when it comes to something of a Spiritual nature; but how can you truly know that you're seeing them accurately? We will go on a brief journey through the energy centers of your body and show you just how you might get in touch with each of them. It is quite important to be connected with these ways as most of them will light up quite strongly when you've connected with your Twin – Flame. Here is a list of the seven Chakras in detail and their functions.

The Crown Chakra: This is located at the top of your head and if you could see it, it would be in the shape of a large circle just like an actual crown. It is the entrance way and also exit point of most if not all of the energy that enters and leaves your body. Think of it as the management center for all of the rest of your energy zones. The Crown Chakra regulates how much energy will come in or go out at one time and determines exactly what area it will go to or leave from.

As complex as you might think it is, the Crown Chakra in fact is quite simple as that is all it does. It is no coincidence that it is located near your brain; but at the same time, it is not merely as complex. The Crown Chakra does take some que's from your brain in the way similar to how the brain regulates blood flow – yet that is where its needs from the brain end. You see, in the most simple of terms, the Crown Chakra is like a pump that pushes water for example through a pipe and at other times like a pump that might need to pour water out. That is the full extent in simple terms of what it does.

The Third Eye Chakra: The Third Eye Chakra allows you the ability to have higher awareness than what is limited by the physical aspects of your body. It is a Spiritual zone which generates uncanny experiences and super human for lack of a better term – knowledge of things that you would otherwise not be able to become aware of. People often say that they can see alternate visions through their third eye and yet it is hard to explain what experiences unless you've had it yourself. Take for example a knowing of certain events and perhaps people that you would otherwise never have knowledge of and yet somehow you find yourself either knowing these things in detail or being quite familiar with the details that are given to you.

When I say a higher knowing, what I also mean is your intuition which you may have heard of. It's the ability to further connect with other energies outside of your body in a way that allows you to peek into the air waves of shared energy and pull out the useful bits that may concern you. There is also a retained knowledge stored here which allow you to bring back memories, sometimes with visually vivid details and it is certainly something to behold if it should happen to present itself. Now, you must know that not everybody will have the same level of ability within their third eye and some may barely have any use of it at all.

It is generally something that you need to develop if you wish to take full advantage of its potential. There are many books circulating regarding the development of your third eye and actually very few of them are accurate. The best way to develop this sensory mechanism is to just allow it to flow, allow all of the things that I've described to come into your awareness when they show up and do not fight them because that will lead to the repression of your instinctual abilities. Most people who have developed their third eye to a good degree have done so through yoga and or meditation.

These two practices allow you if you let them to open up your awareness of the inner workings of your Spiritual – Self. You'll find that practicing these things enables you to be more receptive to a higher enjoyment of your whole body make up and the wonderful, non – physical components that we all have.

The Throat Chakra: The Throat Chakra is the basis for communication. It ebbs and flows in its ability to express your truth in both verbal and non – verbal ways. You may find that when you are not able to speak and share what is truly on your mind that the Throat Chakra is malfunctioning in some way. Perhaps you have some repressed fear or anger which has clogged the smooth flow of energy through this center.

In order to clear this up and allow yourself to express your thoughts and feelings clearly, you must clear away blockages located here.

But how to do that is the question? The simplest way is to allow yourself the freedom of giving yourself the awareness that you're communications will only enhance the smooth flow of your bodily functions. In more simple terms, you can just picture your throat as being this open channel or a tube that is flowing freely in both directions, very much like a large water main. This may certainly take some time to perfect and meditating on it will definitely help; but after a short while, this practice will become an automatic part of your everyday life.

If you have no communication issues it is still quite useful from time to time to practice this method as a form of maintaining open dialogue with everyone around you. It is very vital that your Throat Chakra be functioning properly at all times because it is the one center that if imbalanced can cause the others to malfunction as well. As you can see, it is truly the center of your body and the Spiritual balance that we all need. This point in your energy make up also allows communication between each Chakra and so it becomes quite clear on a higher level why it is so important.

The Heart Chakra: This wonderful energy center controls all of the love and compassion that you may or may not feel in your body. It signifies and expresses the true and Divine love that God has given to us. Any distortion or break down in this area will cause you to not feel the true essence of what God has given to us and in turn will not allow you to properly share it with others. It is the source of all the Divine life within you and it carries this wonderful feeling throughout your sacred body.

It you are ever feeling disturbed or that you have no need to love or be compassionate then it is most likely because your Heart Chakra is suffering from its own illness. Certainly we will all have brief moments when the thought of being loving and kind seems to much to handle; but if it continues on then you know for sure that you have an issue with this most vital energy center. It is how we express joy, elation and uncontrollable feelings of love and without it we could not experience any of these in their true form. If you're finding that these things no longer come easily, then you must rectify this Chakra at once.

To do so, you should envision yourself as a glowing flame of orange; one that is burning hotter and hotter still. Allow it to turn into an inferno, all the while feeling it warm you up in a wonderful way; but yet not so much that it burns you. Practice this for several days and you will see just what an amazing difference it can make. You are at the core of your being, the Heart Chakra and it is everything you need to be in order to follow the Christ Conscious Path.

The Sacral Chakra: This is the learning center of your energy zones. It ties in to the rest of the Chakras and retains your experiences and learning that you've accumulated over your lifetimes. It is here where we often have the most issues like retaining old pain and suffering which we need to release in order to be properly balanced and energetic. This is the collection zone if you will; a sort of dumping ground where all of your old baggage is conveniently placed.

You may find that if you constantly retain negative experiences and thoughts that over time you feel heavier and heavier. The only way to release these feelings is to clear out this Chakra and then not allow it to accumulate so much negative energy. Don't get me wrong; this center is not just for harsh experiences and troubles that you've had; it also retains positive and uplifting ones that may have allowed you to come into this life as a happy individual as well. There will be quite a combination of things that your soul has picked up along the way and as you can see by its name, it holds those things that can be considered sacred to our divinely placed existence.

So what to do if you find yourself feeling heavy in an energetic sense? In order to release those things you do not want here in this collection, imagine yourself on an island of your choice generally a tropical island works best; but do pick one that contains the things and environment that are pleasing to your eye. Stroll through this island and pick up things along the way that are clean and new and play around with all of the exciting aspects of your surroundings. Perhaps you are on a beach with clear blue water in front of you.

Take that all in and enjoy how it makes you feel and at the same time reach into your pockets grabbing the contents inside and emptying them out onto the sand. You'll find that when they appear on the outside, they are no longer hard and ugly; instead, they are just random items that are no longer useful to your well - being. In a matter of moments, they may just disappear before your eyes. Once again, this may take some practice to be effective so you should expect to do this several times before you feel a significant change; especially if you retained much in the way of old baggage.

The Root Chakra: This is the source of all your sensual and intimate relationship energies. It governs how well you react to certain stimuli as it relates to the intimate bonds you may have with another. Often times, there will be a disconnect between how you see yourself in those types of situations and the true reality of what's really happening there. It is essential that you stay in touch with this Chakra if you expect to have a satisfying intimate relationship with your partner.

You must not ignore the various sensations that go on in your core area; that is your groin and related parts because to do so will cause your experiences to be less that satisfactory. What I mean when I say pay attention is to note how the different external stimulations affect not only your sexual area; but also the rest of your body at the same time. You'll find that certain types of sexual pleasure will also reach your head or your toes – it really all depends on how in tune you are. When you are most in touch with this Chakra on a level much deeper than the physical sensations, you will find that sexual pleasure and specifically orgasm becomes a whole body experience; especially when you are with your Twin – Flame.

It opens up a whole new world of enjoyment and pleasure when you are fully in touch with this center and the experience level is not limited to just the times when you are making love. This energy has the ability to flow so feely that you may just have whole body experiences at random times through the day. They will not unfortunately be of orgasmic intensity; but they will bring you an over – whelming feeling of euphoria which you will also feel to some extent in that Chakra. Yet how to clear up this energy center if you feel like nothing is happening there in anyway more than the basic pleasure you may experience?

Imagine a light shinning down upon you and focusing on your groin area in the color of white; see how it penetrates that area and breaks apart any dark particles that might be present. The beam of light may be as gentle or as strong as you feel comfortable with and if you feel that you have much in the way of inadequacy here, you will probably have quite a bit of blockage and so you will want to envision a stronger light. As you do this and it will take several instances depending upon your state; feel the warmth that comes into your groin and allow it to feel pleasurable. It's really a matter of freeing yourself from old experiences that were unpleasant which are signified by the dark clutter and fully allowing yourself to enjoy sexual pleasure without any guilt or shame.

The Base Chakra: The final center connects you with the spirit energy of the earth. If used properly, it provides a way to expel clutter from your energy centers down into the earth where they can be cleansed and purified. It is often not something that one would ever be aware of – this ability to rid yourself of harmful energies through your feet; however, it can be a vital component and indeed should be a regular practice to keep everything else in your energy field flowing smoothly.

Imagine that your Base Chakra which as you might expect is located at your feet, to be an exhaust pipe that can connect into the ground when you need it to. However; it will only work this way when you focus this sort of intent upon it. What you may do in order to facilitate this cleansing perhaps in meditations, is to envision roots coming out of your feet and going three feet or so into the ground and you can have as many as you like. They should be wide and strong for they must hold you erect while expelling the toxins that may have built up over time.

What you'll do next is to envision your body expelling any smog or dark clouds or particles from itself through those roots and into the ground and as you do this, see it working like a pump that just keeps pushing and pushing these things away from you. When you are satisfied that your body is clear, many people will see it as being white at this point, allow the ground to wash your roots clean and at the same time feel this new freshness and lighter state over – come your body. After wards, retract your wonderful roots back into your feet until next time. This process is often referred to as grounding yourself.

As two Twin – Flames reunite, they will find that their energy centers unite as well on each level of awareness to this vitally important union in which the

Twin – Souls connect on each level of the Chakras and will often adjust themselves to be more in line with the other. Remember that at one time both of them were in one soul component and so it stands to reason that when they come together in a physical sense and feel so very connected; it is primarily due to those identical energy centers coming back into form again.

This process does not happen immediately; but will work its way through over time. This time frame will depend upon a number of factors with the primary one being; how far away they are from each other in a Spiritual sense; that is at what point are they currently at along the Christ Conscious Path. The closer they are together, the less time it will take for them to fully align their energy centers and of course the farther away they are, the longer it will take. This concept assumes that the one who is behind remains hard at work in catching up to the other; for if they do not – they will not only never fully align their whole Spirit – Selves; but there may come a point where this union falls apart.

Going further and considering that the two Twin – Flames are closing the distance between them or are even at the same level, there will be nothing short of fireworks to be had when all systems line up and come together like they once were at creation. There will come many situations where for example your Heart Chakras beat in unison and the exact feeling and intensity is felt by both. Somewhat less common; but also happening to most Twin – Flame couples, are shared visions of an unexplainable level. The list can go on and be in various combinations and these are further signs that you're truly reconnecting at the highest level and not merely being together physically. It's very exciting when you get to this point as I have experienced myself and you will always find that new things reveal themselves in this way often when you least expect it.

As you connect energetically as true Twin – Flames; your bodies will become more in tune with each other. The energetic connection is then or feels like it's on fire in the sexual sense. Your fluids, your movement, your excitement are then becoming identical. You may notice that more and more you will climax almost at the exact same time. This is what a true Twin – Flame connection is in the realms of Tantric Energy. The heat you feel and can continue to feel exemplifies that; it's the arousing connective nature when Twin – Fouls unite and collide.

What you must again remember is that your soul's were once one and now they are remembering what each other likes and what will please them best on a more subconscious level. This is why you are not always aware about doing anything differently because it's not always in the motions or actions; but rather in the way that your energies work together. In this type of connection, these things soon become automatic without the intervention of the human aspect. It is one of Gods great gifts to you – to experience this. This is also quite rare and needs to be earned between this couple and Twin – Flame union. This passion and excitement grow as an extension of making love all day; as in the Tantric Sex principles.

Chapter Nine

Myths and Truths

The below list is the most prominently written and shared myths circling the globe currently regarding Twin – Flame connections and attractions. Not only have I come across these and been presented with these, I have also personally tested many of these out as you will read in the next section of this book entitled "My Story." It amazes me just how many myths are present and how many people monopolize off of this and how many are fooled into believing these untruths. The Twin – Flame phenomena has turned more into a monopoly or business for many who put forth these untrue methods to capitalize for their own personal gain, than focusing on the truths and the actual sacred blessing that it is and there are so many who are desperately seeking their true Twin – Flame, that they often fall victim to these falsehoods.

You will notice that I will often use the term true Twin – Flame throughout this book. The reason why as many of you may have guessed is that there are many who feel that they are with or who have met their Twin – Flame; when in fact they have not. It may be a soul – mate, or just someone you are fond of and get along with really well. You must understand that a True Twin – Flame is an unexplainable connection that is rare and out of this world as you are and have been reading in this book.

The number one myth stated is that you can attract your Twin – Flame by sending out the correct energetic frequency or vibrational frequency. In reality, the attraction to your Twin has nothing to do with this energy that you might think you're putting out there. In fact, you're not really putting out any useful energy at all. It is virtually impossible to send energy at a specific frequency like some direct you to do. The energy that you might be emitting from your body is to general and common in nature as this is the energy we all have and are made of; for this to work in this fashion. Can you really measure the frequency of your energy and have you ever been able to do this and know for a fact that you are doing so and that it is actually working? Anyone who knows anything about energy and energy matter would know this to be completely false.

The second point is that you can attract your Twin – Flame by manifesting this idea in your mind. This is an impossibility as you cannot bring anything at all to yourself by just thinking about it and has anything else ever been brought to you or worked out for you exactly the way you wanted it by putting the mere thought of it or the outcome you wish for in the way you wanted it to? There must always be some action involved. It's very much like just thinking that you wish to be a millionaire without taking the steps towards that; it just does not work and you will end up with nothing but disappointment. Another thought to ponder on the millionaire aspect; who doesn't wish to become this and how many of these are in the world? If this theory actually worked, we would all be such.

Humans do not possess the power to think things into reality; that is reserved for the Divine. We are not God and again, we must work for the things we desire. Regarding this manifestation process, have you ever heard of God being a part of it or actually mentioned regarding this process or the Divine; being: Jesus Christ, the Archangels, Angels or any other light beings that support God and Gods laws? I keep seeing the word universe being used and displayed in the place of such. Do you really know what this so called Universe represents? I do not. This entire process eliminates the need for mankind to pray and stay in contact and communion with God. Remember again, it is God that blesses us if he chooses so, to reunite with our true Twin – Flame; I am living proof of this.

The third myth states that you can visualize what your Twin – Flame looks like. There is no way of knowing what your unique partner will look like before you meet them; which also ties back into manifesting them to you. How can you do this for sure when you have no clue what they look like? We do not have the ability to see who they are or where they are from; or any other details about our Twin – Flame. To think this way – that one can envision their mate would again be akin to playing God and there is only one God.

The forth myth and theory states that by restructuring your DNA, you can attract your Twin – Flame. Each Twin – Flame is connected on a Spiritual level alone and is not identified by the physical body. Besides it not being possible to restructure; this attraction is on a much higher and unrelated level anyway. This is abundantly clear since over different lifetimes you would have different bodies and of course if you've met and or attracted; the genetic make up would be different each time and in each lifetime. How is it or would it be possible to use any theory regarding DNA when in each lifetime we have different bodies and different DNA and genetic make up? Do you really think it would be possible for the soul matter to know and recognize one another in this fashion? Soul matter – energy, does not contain DNA or anything that is conducive to the physical body; but is separate from.

The fifth myth is that there is nothing to do or no need to do anything at all to attract your Twin – Flame. This sacred union is a gift from God and is only given to those who earn it by serving Him. To serve means to act. You can never expect that just because you have a Twin – Flame that you will ever meet them just sitting there and merely existing or doing nothing to bring this desire into your life. This fallacy could not be further from the truth.

The sixth most common myth is that your Twin – Flame will come to you in the most ideal of situations. Even though you may reconnect with your Twin – Flame, there will still be some work involved in aligning yourselves so that you are fully compatible once again. Often the two will be in much different Spiritual places in their lives and must work at coming together. You will also find that it is a great probability that one, if not both will be in life situations that are not easily cleared up in order to make this reunion an easy transition.

You are not home free so to speak just because you have reunited with your Twin – Flame. The idea is that the two of you together continue to learn and grow as two separate identities that come together again to be one who then together walk further along the Christ Conscious Path. Your journey as one single entity is over; but moving into and onto the next phase of being two who propel forward together to perfect and make the necessary changes to remain in perfect harmony as true Twin – Flames.

The seventh myth is that every Twin – Flame couple who meet will have an easy life afterwards and all is perfect and well. This is certainly not so. As Twin – Flames are still human, they will experience all of the usual challenges that relationships may face. The only difference is that a Twin – Flame couple will be more able to work through them in a peaceful manner. This is not to say that it will be any easier; but instead that part of this sacred union is the ability to have open and honest communication with each other in the most loving way.

The most common and strongest feature of this union is the best friend bond that holds and cements this sacred bond together. This is what builds the solid foundation and holds firm so the other aspects can come and further build this bond into the strong and unbreakable union that it is meant to be. Open and honest communication as I previously stated, mutual respect and the ability to communicate with one another in the most peaceful ways. There is no need for any of the typical relationship issues to surface and continue to hold.

The eighth myth is that your Twin – Flame will always like the exact same things that you do. While this can be true at times, it is not the deciding factor and does not mean that this person is ideally suited for you. Just because you have originated from the same soul does not mean that your needs and desires on your own personal level are still identical. Keep in mind that in the meantime, several lifetimes apart have transpired with different and unique experiences which characterized the other in their own unique way which may not have been exactly the way yours was or is.

You will though discover that as you reconnect; things about yourself will be uncovered that you never realized existed and the real you will emerge. It is true that when true Twin – Flames come together that unresolved issues, concerns and confusions will surface to be healed. One will draw this out of the other and bring it to the surface. This is where we come to really know who we really are together, the likes and dislikes which then bond together in the most delicate way to form a common dynamic and sacred bond.

The ninth myth and I must admit this one to be very common is that you need to initiate some sacred process in order to allow or attract your Twin – Flame to you. This one always makes me shake my head in every direction imaginable. Again, it is up to God as to who reconnects with their Twin – Flame. You could do all of these activation processes and meditations you want; but they will not do anything to hasten, help or speed up the process. You will have wasted much time and be out of pocket many dollars while still waiting and if by chance you do happen to meet someone; learn very quickly that they are not your true Twin – Flame in the least bit.

It is only through the service of God and walking the Christ Conscious Path diligently that this process may occur – this path is the road to and of perfection. It only stands to reason that the creator of you being God would also be in charge of who your Twin – Flame is as he created you and your other half in the beginning as one sole spirit. Do you think or feel that any of these aforementioned methods will bring, draw or attract your true Twin – Flame to you when none of them include Him? God can never ever be omitted from this process; as again it is He who brings this rare, beautiful and sacred gift to you.

The tenth; but not final myth regarding Twin – Flames is that you must change who you are in order to find your Twin – Flame. With or without the desire to meet your Twin – Flame, you should never be anyone other than who you really are. This too, is a gift from God and it is who He wants us to be. So why would He want you to change that for any reason – especially in order to meet your Twin – Flame who is your identical Spirit match? You were identical in the beginning and will be again after your personal discovery together so why would you want to or have to change for anyone?

If this is a prerequisite to be with anyone; you should not be with them and they are most certainly not your true Twin – Flame. Do you not think that if God brings you two together that he will see it to be fit, right and Divine and that with your continued service and diligence to Him that he will over – see the perfection of the two souls that he once created as one? God equals perfection and with your participation and service of Him and to Him he most certainly will give you and guide you to your very own perfection with your true Twin – Flame.

Some other points to ponder that I have seen repeatedly rather it be on youtube, websites, articles; or elsewhere are as follows: The awakened one walking in life will feel connected to their Twin – Flame; one is awake and the other is not. This is really irrelevant as often times Twin – Flames are here reincarnated on earth at the same time; but do not meet or reunite because it has not been earned by either one or both parties. Has it been proven that one is awakened and one is not? One has to have earned this gift and be walking steadfastly on the Christ Conscious Path to earn this gift; but it can also be possible that both are on the same path and walking in the same direction.

Another point I often see stated is that if one Twin – Flame does not work out and is not ready that another one comes along with an equal vibrational frequency. This one I would think is self – explanatory in its falseness. As we all know there is only one true Twin – Flame for each human being. God did not create one being that was split into three; but rather two; hence the term twin. Ask yourself now how it would be possible for another to have a matching vibrational frequency to the one who is ready; this point also deflates the vibrational frequency theory yet again as well.

The truth of the matter is that it is possible that a soul – mate who in definition is a soul who you knew in a past life; but is not your Twin – Flame can come along and be very close or so it would seem to fitting the bill of your Twin – Flame. God will bring to you your exact

Twin – Flame when and if you have earned it and as He sees fit. The one who may have not been ready as it is written is not your true Twin – Flame. Do you honestly think that God in all His perfection, grace, mercy and love would bring along this sacred and rare gift to you if you were both not ready for it?

I have also seen it written or heard it verbally spoken that holding the vibrational frequency of unconditional love and accumulating the knowledge through appropriate research are the prerequisites for reuniting with your Twin – Flame. Unconditional love is a lifestyle and practicing thereof; it is not a vibration or a frequency. I am to understand then that this means that your energy just has to hold this vibration? Does that make sense to you? On the point of accumulating enough knowledge to qualify in meeting your Twin - Flame I would also like to point out that the source that stated this also stated that what you need to do was to let go and just live your life and wait after laying out many prerequisites. My first question to myself was Well which one is it now? Are we supposed to do all of these things or just sit and wait and live our lives?

Much of what I have seen regarding the topic of reuniting with your Twin – Flame was rather confusing and very contradictory. I highly suggest to you that when you review some or all of the material out there in circulation regarding your Twin – Flame; that you review each and every point stated and I can guarantee you that you will almost always find at least one contradiction. Another point is that none of the resources I have seen stated anywhere that they were with their own true Twin – Flame so how is it that they may have any expertise on this subject and if they are offering this sort of advice regarding Twin – Flames; I can also assure you that they are not with their Twin – Flame. Have you ever asked yourself this question? All of that which I write in this book is based on my own experiences with my own true Twin – Flame and one of the main reasons why I decided to write and publish this book to share with others. We cannot offer our opinion or expertise on any topic if we have not personally lived or experienced it.

The facts remain quite clear that none of these so called methods are of any use in attracting your Twin – Flame. There's only one simple way to accomplish this goal and that is to follow the Christ Conscious Path now and always. There are no short cuts, no gimmicks; no energetic vibrations that will push you closer to your Divine Twin. You cannot avoid the fact that God is the sole decision maker as to who reconnects with their Twin – Flame and who does not. It's really quite simple, don't you agree? Many hours and days and weeks will be saved, not to mention many dollars if you just follow the simple ways of being blessed with your Twin – Flame that are described in this book.

Conclusion

Explore all of the option available to you in finding your Twin – Flame and then see why none of them will work. Many have been inundated with false information and concepts that are not based on any facts. Often enough, these systems of attracting your Twin – Flame tend to be confusing at best. They deal with topics that very few actually understand and end up leaving the followers even more lost than before. The truth is that in order to find your Twin – Flame, you must follow very specific and yet simple guidelines that center around serving God; there is no other way. If someone enters your life outside of this simple fact; they are not your Twin – Flame. And I don't mean going to church. You have to have good intentions as a human being it's really that simple.

You saw exactly what a genuine Twin – Flame relationship is and be able to recognize your own with in depth facts and truths. See for yourself how much sense this straight forward text can make to you on your journey to finding your own genuine Twin – Flame.

It is my hope that after reading through the text in this book that you now know exactly what a twin – flame relationship is and exactly how to go about finding yours. If all things are not in play, then you will not find your twin – flame. Make a check list to see if you have all the qualities of such a relationship. And remember in following God and the Christ Conscious path you have to be an outstanding citizen and a good person.

Oh what an amazing book! It has cleared up so many confusing questions I have had regarding Twin – Flames and has set me straight with a clear mind. After wasting so much time with those other popular and misleading methods, it's nice to finally have the real story and to make sense of it all. What a joy this book was to read!

Joanne Wilkinson (MA) Marriage and Relationships Counselor

Poetry

Please take and use this poetry to share with your twin – flame. And fall in love like never before. Poetry written by Dr. Angela Heppner.

A Hearts Yearning

You speak to my heart, loved me from the very start
You speak to my soul, helping me to feel whole
I love you baby, you sure know how to drive me crazy
I desire and crave every single bit of you, because you're you

Eternity is unfathomable to most, spoken as just a word
You and I know what it is; our prayers have been heard
You tickle me on the inside so deep down within
Waking every inch of me, exuberant with that sultry grin

The words I love you just don't seem enough or right
A love like ours, outshines the starriest night
No words can come close to the way I feel about you
You are a priceless gem in all you say and do

Together before, always, and here we are once more
Connected as we've always been, so much to adore
On a blissful journey once again to finish what we started
You and I both know though, that we never really parted

Hold me oh so tight treasure me, don't ever let me go
As each day passes by, our love can't help but to grow
You motivate, inspire, and play with that little girl inside of me
Bring peace, true love, faith and hope to me, our blissful destiny

A Love Like Ours

How you inspire me
Make my dreams come true
My entire eternity has been spent
In search of and only loving you

I adore you beyond words to speak
A love like ours can only be felt by the meek
It's a love that never dies but lives on and on
Penetrating our two hearts leading us to where we belong

Your love is stronger than a mother's love
Deeper than the deepest sea
I thank the heavens every day
That this love has been given to me

How long I spent waiting and hoping
Just existing, most times merely coping
My heart and soul rejoice that your love is finally here
I look forward to sharing my life with you year after year

You bring out that little girl inside of me
And fill her with so much love
She feels so at peace and free to be
With the one and only man she has ever deeply loved

Nothing can break a love like ours
It's a love that never dies
Felt in the hearts by two for eternity
Our most precious and sacred love
Is written for us in the skies

A Lovers Tale

The epitome of a dream come true
It's the love story of me and you
Written in the stars, glistening like angels
That of fate, destiny, a love like no other
An untouchable love, one filled with the utmost purity

Brought into this world to start over again
Not knowing our purpose, sometimes feeling grim
Hoping beyond all odds to find our one true love
One that could touch us deeply, recognize our beauty
Love us for who we are, fill that void within our hearts

Love at first site; I believe it to be true
One look into your eyes was all it took, I had the answer
The earth let go beneath me, my whole foundation shook
That bright light of love and passion in your eyes
The light of hope, and fulfillment brought tears to mine

You touch me so deeply with your unconditional love
There to guide me, love me, support me, catch me when I fall
Your warm eyes penetrate mine, making me feel like I have it all
A blessed and beautiful soul, you complete me, make me feel whole
You my love are the perfect match for my soul

I want to tell you now and always how very much I love you
You're the love of my life, my very own dream come true
You breathe life into me and want to be a part of my destiny
You share my dreams and help me to be all I can be
Above all, you have shown me that I can be loved for me

For All Eternity

I'm guilty of a divine love in the first degree
The recipient of such love is you handsome baby
Your precious heart melts me into endless pieces
You're the striking subject of my favorite thesis

Engrossed in your adorning eyes and lengthy lashes
You could knock me down and I would feel no gashes
The earth could crumble and fall in and I wouldn't care
As long as you're by my side with your adorning stare

The birds sing a melodious song made of me and you
The blue star shines and signifies all we are and do
You hold me and touch me like you did years ago
Looking down on me, my hair in your hands; a golden glow

I have written so many poems before to the man with no face
That man was you now in my life; that nothing can replace
You set my heart aflutter all the while you start to stutter
The sweetest divine duo we are; sweeter than milky butter

You could hold me forever and never ever let me go
I love the way you touch me; such undying love you show
Your everyday is my heaven, solace and blissful paradise
Together the perfect couple, I am the fire and you the ice

Always Been You

There are a dime and dozen and then only a few
So many valid reasons why I am in love with you
You are the man of my dreams and the one for me
No questioning it; even the blind could plainly see

How I adore your precious smile and sultry eyes
Your playful nature and super charming demise
The romantic I have always known that is you
Admiring everything about you and all that you do

A passionate spirit flaming as the hot summer sun
It has only ever been you; for me you are the only one
Created masterfully from the very beginning of time
You are the light in my heart for you I'll always shine

All the many years you have been away from me
My heart in search of the perfect love of thee
How blessed I am to finally be reunited with you
I could not wait to finally be able to say I do

Anything and everything belongs to you and only you
There is nothing in the world for my sweet love that I wouldn't do
I never knew perfect until the very first time I set eyes on you
And now no one in the world comes close to the perfection of you

You are the gladiator and true man that the world has sadly lost
The only one of few left who comes to the world at no cost
Your heart is pure, yet wiser and more intuitive than any other
Your arms, lips and perfect softness are always worth a smother

There are many pretty faces in this sad and often cruel world
Yours is definitely one of them, yet yours is the real deal
What you see is what you will always get, you're so very real
You're beauty inside and out; it's so obvious you need only feel

Aphrodisiacal Sex

It all starts with some romantic fun during the day
Not allowing any precious moment to slip away
Touching my shoulder as you walk on by
Lying on the ground with me to watch the sky

Picking a delicate flower to put in my hair
Gazing at me intensely with a loving stare
Going into public skirted and no underwear
Always the perfect gentleman, pulling out my chair

So sexy, delicious and appeasing you are
Anywhere with you my love; even in the car
Kissing your neck and devouring your soul
A little strip tease in the night up against the pole

Sweet yet sultry whispers into your alert ears
Wanting you to ravish me year after year
That erogenous spot made for just me and you
Right down at the bottom, one little tickle will do

A hot kiss, rub, some caressing here and there
A hot oil massage committed with tender loving care
Caressing my breasts you get the passion going
Non- stop attraction boiling and now over - flowing

How I desire your manhood thrusting up against me
Rubbing and probing; such naughty erotic fantasy
The way you tease me with your divinely made tool
Hotter and more alert than ever, he really isn't a fool

You take me from behind with such erotic loving care
Admiring my curvy back with such a sultry stare
That passion in your eyes, the tiger roaring about
Gnashing and gnawing; oh he wants to come out

Your sexy smile silhouetting the hot satin sheets
What we got baby surely is not for the meek
Your responsive body off the tip of my wet tongue
Enraged manhood desperately now seeking some fun

Moaning and groaning; begging me not to stop

Twin Flame Truths   Dr. Angela Heppner

I slip my petite hands right over your hottest spot
Licking, grabbing and lavishing, missing no part of you
All night long baby until you are barking at the moon

A cataclysmically beautiful wonderful seismic event
The perfect amount of friction and we're both spent
This is not just a dream it's much better than that one
After volcanic release, the most natural high has been won

Baby I Love Your Ways

Whether I am awake or asleep
My love for you runs so deep
You have my heart more than I know
With every beat it continually grows

The love I have for you that is
The feelings for you continue to fizz
How I love to lie in your warm embrace
It's always been you, no one can replace

I really did not think you would ever come
So I let go and continued alone into the sun
Now that you are here my heart can't let go
I would do almost anything for you as you know

How I adore your babbling and quirky ways
Your breath taking smile saving the day
It so hard to describe this perfect love we have
The only way I can do this is to say I am

We are just molded perfectly it's so plain to see
This love that has continued on even into eternity
So now that you are gone my heart is terribly sad
Broken into delicate pieces from once being so glad

Oh how sad I was to see you part and walk away from me
Tears coming down my cheeks out of my eyes of the sea
I know you will return and I look forward to that day
In the meantime having trust and faith in God to pave our way

Colors of the Rainbow

Forever has just now begun
Two hearts melting in the sun
When I look at you I come un-done
Radiant, passionate and so much fun

You're a cosmic burst of pure energy
Symbolic of all that love should be
A gorgeous rainbow shining through
I could make a living out of loving you

My heart dances and skips a beat
Magically swept me off my feet
I only have one vision and it's you
My only wish is to see this through

Walls of defense crashing the ground
You snuck right in without making a sound
Caught in your smile and lost in your eyes
You're the closest to heaven there's no disguise

You are the ocean and I am the waves
Merging together; like putty and clay
Orange, yellow, pink, green, red and blue
In the English alphabet we are the
I am so deeply smitten and into you

Damn Hot Chemistry

I can't wait to get my hands all over your body
It's not a booty call but some damn hot chemistry
Us together is like a day with no weather
But you can assure yourself, I've got the feather

I am so completely head over heels in love with you
That I go insane a little each day and don't know what to do
So I sit here and think of all that I can do to please you
Sexually and otherwise is all really that I want to do

Our bodies together wrapped in the sweetest sweat
Boy, am I ever glad that fate said I think it's time you met
You can call me your toy, play thing or otherwise
You send me straight to the moon and staring at the skies

Pick up the phone and call me baby right now
The performance you're about to get requires a bow
If I couldn't touch you or make love to you I would surely go mad
The things you do in and out of the bedroom sure make me glad

I've got what you need and you've got what I need
Now get down under the covers and plant that hot seed
I'll never say no to you and will always be at the ready
Come here you and touch my body and turn it into putty

We've got the hot, the desirable and the super perfect love
I swear to God that it had to only of come from above
How else does this master of perfection that is us transpire?
Who cares, get out the glasses and let's get going for hours

Destiny's Home

A life long journey lost and confused
In search of something, yet we could not see
Never giving up, yet never feeling completely whole
Looking for a place to call home one nourishing to our souls

Faith has kept me, kept me holding on
Longing, waiting, desiring, for a love that strong
A love like no other, a home for my soul
God heard my prayers, he sent you to me
The greatest blessing of all, what my soul needed to make it whole

A great blessing of the Universe, that of destiny
A love so pure and utterly flawless
One of mystery, deep drawn out desires
That's the love of you and me

Those eyes of yours so beautiful and true
Touch so deep down within me
Grasping and shaking every fiber of my being
That feeling of peace and harmony
It's within your eyes, the window to your soul
In there for me to reap the rewards of those only I can see

Eyes that melt me, bring me to my knees
A familiarity that is only unique and special to me
That warm feeling; a feeling of a past life and destiny
A look of contentment; one that completes me

The undying and eternal souls of two
How grateful I am for the love I found in you
I'm elated to have found you once again my love
You are again completing me, loving me, nurturing me
Giving me my souls needs and desires, setting my inner being on fire
Thank you for loving me as you do; making all my dreams come true

Divine Love

The blissful reunion of a love never broken
Energies soaring, not one word spoken
Fairies, angels, delightful musical sounds
The singing Angels were always bound

Rock solid created from the beginning
Time after time the two come out winning
ESP, Telepathy, Astral World, Intuitions
Yin and Yang; the strongest connection

Connected in each and everyway
You are the putty and I am the clay
Both gifted with the gift of voice
Neither one ever had a choice

A prince and a princess a story to tell
When one looked at the other they both fell
Love at first site raising the bluest seas
The dynamic duo has been in place for eternity

Perfect dance partners always have been
Both can sing a beautiful song in perfect unity
Given the same gifts right from the very start
Two solid flames bearing a solid golden heart

The white horse is coming the trumpets sound
Energies fully alive shaking the ground
Nothing can break this its' already been tried
God won't allow this; it's written it in the skies

Electrified

You're my oasis in the desert
My island in the sun
The one I dream of often
For me, you are the one

You are the gem within my crown
Such a treasure to behold
Your love bears no comparison
It is worth much more than gold

You are always deep within me
Even in times of deep distress
How my heart grows ever fonder
When I feel your warm caress

I close my eyes and I think of your kiss
Every minute apart it's you that I miss
You have touched my heart in a special way
I am thankful I found you each and every day

My body shivers when I feel your touch
You smell so good I adore you so much
You have an angelic smile, such a kind soul
You are the one I think about, my life is so full

It's the beauty inside that I love to see
That by far is most important to me
Just to know that you will always be there
No one in this world could ever compare

Haven't Met You Yet

I know who you are, yet we've never even met
You're the one I've been longing to love and pet
The one who steals my breath away no fail
It's you and I who have the greatest tale

Your looks don't really matter at all to me
But I do love long hair and curls you see
Maybe some hands that know how to caress
Kisses long and tender, hair a tussled mess

Fate hasn't been all that kind to the two of us
We're more likely to cross the street and hit a bus
And yet I feel it could still happen and we could meet
Maybe in a cafe or a busy dance club with sweet beats

I want you to know that it's you and always has been
This girl has been waiting oh so long, it's not a dream
Stop just sitting there and wishing and hoping
Down to the bottom of a bottle merely just coping

Start looking and get up and out and off that chair
Be sure to wear your most revealing underwear
Because my sexy someone I will be waiting
You can do as you wish including some baiting

I'll be the girl with the biggest smile on her face
When I see you there will be no distaste
Baby come to me and find me, I am still here
Waiting, pondering and thinking year after year

We'll have the best time I swear it to you
Who knows I might even be wearing blue
I'll take it off and even wonder to put it back on
I will be the girl who is willing to write you a song

Heaven Scent

My heart pulsating; a raging desire
My soul alive and fully on fire
The first time my eyes saw you
My sweetest dream came true

You are the rose in full bloom
Radiance of a bright full moon
Your beauty never leaves me
Turquoise waters in the bluest sea

Tingling right from head to toe
Such unfathomable love you sow
Sheer delight on a cold winter's night
Eyes that shine of breathe taking light

A beautiful soul that continually glows
A scent of heaven planted row after row
Your love will soar freely for all to see
Not to be caged; but left to simply be

Your energy speaks of delicate grace
A gentle touch that nothing can replace
A best friend and lover until the end
You my love; a blissful and true Godsend

Home Sweet Home

All of my life I've drifted and wandered, often feeling grim
In search of a heart much like my own, a place to engross myself in
Thinking I knew what I wanted, knowing what was best
Life came along and carried me away putting me to the test

Then one day it all hit me a love that took me by storm
A love unfathomable to man, one to keep me warm
As if struck by lightning my whole existence shook
Wake up angel it's time you take a good hard look

A soul awoke, as if living and breathing for the first time
The man of my dreams right before me, wanting to be mine
Loving, desiring sharing with me for oh so long
Giving his all to me so I don't have to be so strong

Nothing compares to you baby, you tickle my soul
Reaching deep within me, you make me feel warm and whole
Whatever it takes, whatever we need to do
I want to spend the rest of my days with you

In Every Delicate Rose

My love is like an ocean
It goes down so deep
My love is like a rose
Whose beauty you want to keep

My love is like a river
That will never end
My love is like a dove
With a beautiful message to send

My love is like a song
That goes on and on forever
My love is like a mountain
It's you and I that raise above

You are everything to me
A soul and spirit, touching mine
I never knew such beauty existed
Until the day I met you

I wrote your name in the sky
But the wind blew it away
I wrote your name in the sand
But the waves washed it away
I wrote your name in my heart
And forever it will stay

All the love that the world may know
Is said to be in every rose
Yet all that could be found in two
Is less than what I feel for you

I do believe that God above
Created you for me to love
He chose you from all the rest
Because he knew I could love you best

Indescribable One

Soft, warm eyes being the loving soul of you
Brilliant blue eyes deeper than the bluest blue
A match made in heaven, foreseen, destined to be
An answered prayer, a journey set in motion for all eternity

A love unfathomable, one that glistens like the morning dew
One indescribable, so sacred only to be treasured by a precious few
One heart feels, the other one feels the same, automatically knowing
Instinctively stepping in to keep the other nurtured and growing

Any imaginable emotion, buried, hidden deep down inside
Picked up and brought out by the other, impossible to hide
Unspoken words of love, hope, encouragement, a solid foundation
No words necessary, more than enough love to cement a nation

A love that speaks for itself, far surpassing the words I love you
Each one knowing this exquisite love is only meant for the two
One that can't possibly be shared with everyone they love
For it's meant for them to embrace and share the blessing from above

Leaving this world to return once more, again in search of each other
To find this love , much more powerful than the love of a mother
Two souls find each other yet again, always destined to be together
Beating all, braving the storm, conquering the stormiest of weather

A love like this, never parishes, disappears or fades away
This love is fate, purity and holiness, life after life, it's here to stay
One look at each other, that mystical love rekindles on its own
Here together to grow, love once again, until we find our way home

Lifetime's Repeated

Together as friends once before, the past had been unfair
The timing just wasn't right, for two pure hearts to share
Two souls that mirror each other, a love that's never done
Time would tell if they would reconnect to beat blissfully as one

A blessing given from heaven for you and I to see
A passion never felt before a delicious sensuality
A long hard road, tried, tested, growing into our own
As fate would have it the heavens open, a miracle is shown

Romantic, passionate, two hearts and souls filled with love
As pure as the white rose, more delicate than a dove
A love signifying a fairy tale, a precious dream come true
The pearly gates opened up its doors and brought me to you

Everything in common a natural love has transpired
Fate, destiny, an answered prayer, two hearts on fire
The world is now so magical, peace residing within
A perfect match made in heaven, life's no longer grim

True love expresses itself; she loves her man with all her heart
He loves every inch of her; he knew that from the start
She is his angel, free to be the one she truly is
Her heart beats in perfect rhythm so happy to be his

The Only Girl in the World

Sensations rushing far out of control
You're so special; oh how I love you so
You tickle me right from the inside out
It has always been you; not one doubt

To the very end of the earth and back
This is the best kind of heart attack
You reach right in and stir me up
Never seem to fail to fill my cup

You spin me around and upside down
Only pure love exists; no time for a frown
Feeling like I'm the only girl in the world
A giant ice cream with the prettiest swirl

You rock me and touch my body like no other
Oh how I desire you there could never be another
This far surpasses what fairytales are made of
You thrill me to no end giving my heart such a shove

Your eyes speak to mine like a language unknown
You are within me; I feel you so deep within my bones
To hold you in my arms and feel you; oh so desirable
I am in way over my head in the best way possible

Lost In Your Eyes

I get completely lost in your far beyond beautiful eyes
Breath taking beauty; delicate charm, no hidden disguise
Angels dancing, shining a blinding and bright golden light
A once in a lifetime blessing sent on a dark cold night

I see me in your eyes; my heart, deepest desires, my reflection
No doubting this powerfully crazy and magnetic connection
I could spend forever gazing into your astonishing eyes
You hypnotize and paralyze me; rip me apart inside

Being pulled in, twisted and turned; shot off my heels
Your eyes tell me that this love is so true and so real
Captured by the moon, being pulled in deeply by the tide
Drawn into you way deep down into those radiantly pure eyes

It's not the breath taking color, the shape or magnificent size
Tugging at my heart; my destiny is waiting in your eyes
There is an unexplainable security and comfort; my home
It's you and me baby stepping into the mysterious twilight zone

Every time I try to rise above, you pull me in with your love
That feeling I get, that powerful awe can only be sent from above
There's just no escaping that deep passionate love within your eyes
You're the love of my life with that heaven sent precious demise

Your eyes never leave me, so engrained deeply within me
I see them everywhere, beautifully shining and embellished with care
They are the candle that lights my way beckoning my heart to stay
So hard I try, can't keep my eyes off of you; just one more gaze

I see my every wish and dream come true swimming in your eyes
I see a love beyond all love, purity, bliss; nothing resembling a lie
Hearts, butterflies, an angelic aura, everything magical on the planet
Oh this is getting to me; I know you're my true love, I just can't stand it

Sleep with your eyes open so I can have just one more glance
I am head over heels for you; in over my head, never stood a chance
Reflections of us dancing to our own song painted in the skies
Two hearts together in a fairytale found within each other's eyes

Loves' Finest Mix

My love for you never ends and goes on and on
The perfect artist of my favorite and finest song
To think and know we were identical in the beginning
I fought so hard against all odds just to come out winning

Never gave up on you, our bond or our precious love
The one meticulously and magically made by God above
My heart ached in an everlasting and unending search for you
Not once letting go of all we were, are and used to do

That Cinderella I know I was and wanted to be
It was not just a silly dream or great big wish you see
You set the precedence for that one; my heart so full
Planting delicately picked roses in my garden to grow

You romanced me endlessly filling my days with passion
Never let me down and treasured me in greatest fashion
Reading from the book of your heart you filled me with glee
Carrying me on your arm with pride for the world to see

I simply cannot put words to the way you make me feel
A love like ours and your precious heart is so very real
Our fairytale romance is much more than a dream come true
Forever may not be long enough for me to spend in love with you

The flowers you picked and placed so lovingly in my hair
Fixing my dress and corset you always had such a fine flair
That handsome and dashing Prince with the long dark curls
Holding me so lovingly as we danced; with a passionate whirl

Those are just a few things and only to name a few
This is the lifetime I love to make new memories with you
So many I have already liked watching the clouds roll on by
You and I amazed at all the beautiful shapes we saw in the sky

You holding me against that tree oh what a precious memory
My hair blowing in your face was our only care and reality
The romantic and oh so passionate picnic on the beach that day
Laying on a blanket with you and watching the stars at play

The nightly massages you give to me with your sensual hands

Twin Flame Truths   Dr. Angela Heppner

The way you gaze into my eyes far surpasses all beautiful lands
Your sultry smile that teases me at your bratty and playful times
You hold the key to my heart and make my divine bells chime

The beautiful tears you shed when we reminisce together
Our hopes and dreams pushing through the stormy weather
The way you stutter when you are lost inside our love
How cute is that; to me it's the greatest gift from above

The friendship I have always wanted but never found or had
Is with you my best friend, confidant and lover and boy I'm glad
That I found and have all these beautiful and rare things with you
Because not just any man and certainly not the fake Prince's will do

As hard as they try, they never came close to holding a candle to you
They were not my everlasting and dynamic Prince and would not do
My heart knew that you were the one for me and decided to wait
God has shown such grace upon me; now I know the meaning of fate

You are so gorgeous inside and out at times I just want to shout it out
This is my Prince; the one I knew was my true love without a doubt
He treats me like the lady I am; loving me no fail, taking my hand
Spoiling me and putting my needs first; writing my name in the sand

You hold my heart and hold me so tightly that I cannot see or breathe
Eyes closed and heart wide open; you are the only one I can truly see
I am trapped in your web of sultry, romantic, passionate and pure love
Two golden rings, many golden harps and the wings of a white dove

Our love is the love that no one understands and most will never
Figure it out long enough to earn their own love or even get it together
I do not mind however because this love is sacred and just for two
The ones who can rejoice in this divine blessing are welcome too

You set the finest example for what a man should truly be made of
Outside and in you are the divine meaning of a loyal mans love
I would write your name in the stars and sail the stormiest of seas
To bask in your love and show the world what you mean to me

Loves Perfection

Is not only an outer physical beauty
But a penetrating inner splendor
That glows deep within the chambers of the soul
And brightly radiates through all impediments
Forsaking any and all boundaries

It is not visible perfection
The perfection lies embedded in
The melding of two hearts, two souls
To richly create an everlasting bond
That survives through all imperfections
Surpassing all and a moment in time

Is not a brilliant raging fire
But the kind of warmth one feels
From a peaceful golden fire's glow
An incomparable and unfathomed comfort
In the face of adversity and despair
An offering of deeply penetrating hope
When all appears and is rendered hopeless

Is the love of you and I
With two hearts and souls
A warm brilliant glowing light
Everlasting faith and hope
Together conquering the world
As one heart and one soul
I love you now and always

My Dashing Prince

My Prince, My Prince you have come to me!
So long I've awaited your return
Waiting and lost in an eternity
Watching flowers bloom along the way
Chasing the others who thought
They were you up and away

There is not one who could ever take your place
Not one who much like you could
Set my heart on fire and make it race
You take me in the night; screaming
Moans of ecstasy and sheer delight
You hold me and caress me so tenderly
In the day – chasing all the blues away

240 years I have waited for you to hold me
Once again and hold me oh so dear
Looking, praying, searching and hoping
Yet knowing none of the others were you
They all wanted to be and thought they were
But only you know how to love these curves

A Princess knows in her heart who her Prince really is
He is the one who tickles her fancy
And sends her straight into a roaring fizz
Only he knows exactly how to touch her
The right way in all the right places
Capturing her glance every moment with
His deep, erotic and fiery gazes

He is the one who will capture the sun
And see to it that all of her days are full of fun
He breeds her a special flower representing
Something symbolic of her beautiful heart and soul
Does everything and anything to ensure that
She always remains pure, glorious and whole
He bathes her and brushes her silky hair
Showering her in his tender loving care

Drenches her in fragrant blossoming flowers every hour
Whisks her away repeatedly, such charismatic power

Walking humbly beside her fanning her frame
While she skips and saunters down the streets
Never failing for a moment to sweep her off her feet
He never squanders and always has the most
Loving gaze upon her when she wanders

He lay beside her at night with one eye open
Gazing upon her beauty with sincerest devotion
He is the one dashing, charming knight who
Makes loves to her morning, noon and night
For he knows that she is the lovely one
She is the one and only sweet love of his life

Not only are you a Prince in stature and name
But royalty has since before lived in your veins
You were my Prince in lifetimes before
Royalty in a castle, back to love me once more
There were others; but only you are the one for me
It was and is you I am so crazy and madly in love with
You are the one who melts me and shares in my sweet destiny

Will you caress me and hold me forever? I never want you to stop
As time passes this timeless romance just gets hotter than hot
Your gorgeous magnetic eyes and rich, thick eyelashes
Catch me of guard; giving me constant hot flashes
Those special and sacred moments are yours my dashing Prince
I have followed my heart and here you now are
My sweetest wish came true and now we are back to the start

My Last Breath

My Prince, my Prince where for art thou?
So long I have waited for thee to come
Feeling, hearing, knowing of my love for thee
Searching for you in the eyes of others

But you were not they and they not you
Expressing my love for you through my written words
Living the joy and love for you here in my heart
Picking fragrant flowers and dreaming as we used to do

This handsome Prince of mine is where the sun shines
Oh my darling love, how I have missed you so
The nights and days running freely in my heart
Your tender lips and touch upon my skin

How long I have wished and prayed for you to appear
By the grace and love of God you are here
To pick up where we left off; an un-finished love story
Left waiting in the wings and drifting endlessly on pause

So much love in my heart for you to adore and re-claim
Our romantic days and passionate nights – a delicate rain
Now that you have returned to me we finished where we left off
This time guided and loved by fate – beating all the odds

Now I write and share the very depths of my heart with you
For you are the dashing Prince I once loved with my being and knew
Cinderella and her sweetest dreams have now come true
To spend all of my days adoring, embracing and loving only you

My Love Is Your Love

Here I sit warmly; dreaming of you
Trying to write, wondering what to do
How can I ever put down on paper
A response to your heart of loves vapor

The words you express to me thrill me
In the best ways possible; oh my baby
What you do to me inside and out
Touching me deeply without a doubt

Your poetic words are written in the stars
One in a million gifted you truly are
Your love and passion pouring out of you
You drive me crazy, that is what you do

To have and to hold from this day forward
The way you love me is way over board
You make those others all look like fools
When I look at you I can't help but drool

The say actions speak louder than words
When it comes to you; this is just absurd
For I know your heart speaks a sacred love
One that is only connected to God above

Day in and day out you set me on fire
In this same way it's only you I desire
It is said that love always finds a way
With us it just is and will always stay

My Precious One

Your subtle deep passionate stare
In my dreams, in the bedroom, everywhere
Your penetrating touch leaves me waiting more
In the forest, under the stars, and living room floor

How I crave your soft, wet lips on me
Climbing the walls – a one way ticket to eternity
Thighs quivering – day, night and afternoon delight
You drive me insane my dashing man of the night

I awaken in the morning with you right next to me
Your warm body on mine – what a sight to see
Pulsating hearts beating and rocking in tune
Flowing juices pollinating the flowers in June

You get me going before I even open my eyes
Dropping hot sweat and flashing your passionate demise
There is no morning, noon or night with you
Anytime and any place is all it takes and we do

You've got me going, all fired up inside
Splishing and splashing; ready to take a dive
On my mind every minute of each and every day
Heart skipping a beat – I really have no say

When you touch me I forget my name
Oh my handsome one – you're driving me insane
Gritting my teeth, can't keep my hands off of you
Teasing me senselessly – I just don't know what to do

You sneak up behind me, I don't see you coming
Chase me around the bedroom – I won't be running
There is no struggle; I surrender with smiles and glee
Lashing me with your tongue – driving me to my knees

Oh my love you drive me so crazy
When you rock my world and call me baby
I'm not going anywhere; but straight into your arms
Spending a life sentence basking in your charm

Our Divine Union

Our love touches the deepest seas
Outliving the length a eternity
I adore you and all you've come to be
You commit and pledge your love unto me
My heart embraces the strength of yours
Our love touches from shore to shore

It takes time for a love so precious to grow
Ours took no time at all; already there to sow
To be united and brought together as one
Divine from the beginning; brighter than the sun
Ecstatic to be; though we've never parted

I cannot breath, you're all I see
Delicate hair blowing in the breeze
Deep sensual, passionate kisses
Sweet, soft and tender caresses

Always and forever on my mind
You are the only sun that shines
How fair and beautiful thou art
An arrow of love through my heart

No escaping this precious destiny
Again and again, it's only you I see
I'm a prisoner to your gorgeous eyes
Your smile, a breath taking sunrise

Love embedded deep within my soul
The water that makes my garden grow
Lips that can sink a thousand ships
Nothing can send this pure love adrift

I miss you and you're not even gone
Your precious love is my only song
My yesterday, tomorrow and today
Silhouettes dancing now and always

You've got the shake, rattle and roll
I have the key to your precious soul
Your passionate, romantic soul has me

Twin Flame Truths   Dr. Angela Heppner

Eyes fairer than the bluest of all seas

A perfect match; we are quite the catch
The others before you just didn't match
You have my mind, heart, body and soul
You are the spark in my life; my glistening glow

Painted Picture

My heart calls out to you in sincerest devotion
Pounding rushing colorful waves on the ocean
Nothing is deep enough to house my love for you
I am fully emerged in everything that you do

I saw your face shining on the brightest star
My only desire is to be exactly where you are
Your silhouette follows me everywhere I go
Empowering love, swimming in your passionate soul

Your eyes don't leave me engrained in my mind
I would do anything for you, even remove time
Come forth to me dancing in loves joyous light
You are my joy of the day and love of the night

Your love has consumed me and swallowed me whole
To give back and paint the picture of the love you bestow
Would take a lifetime so pure and magical without end
Your name on my heart for an eternity I will spend

Perceptive Sexes Right in Tune

The red hot flame that burns within
To hot to handle, such delicious sin
Burning under the hearts warmer
Will not go out; does not even smolder

Take my breath away, show me what you got
I'm going to find it whether you like it or not
Want to play a game of hide and seek?
The tigress is waiting; she isn't so meek

Over to the right the facet of utter delight
Your place or mine; let's rock the night
Don't be shy, meet me halfway
You are the putty, I am the clay

Anywhere with you, there is no depends
The start of a passionate night that never ends
A deep connection found within each others eyes
To genuine and mind boggling to disguise

Breaking down the door, can't wait to get in
That sweet scent of your hot and sweaty skin
Two hearts that will never be tamed
Touch me, say my name; say my name

The rooms' ablaze satin sheets from white to red
To mesmerized to catch what the other one said
Silhouettes in abundance, sweet sound of chimes
The hour doesn't matter; there is no place and time

He whispers; I feel I've known you in another life
She gives him a sultry smile knowing that he's right
A connection and bond from lifetimes before
In place for the two of them to fully adore

They put the P in passion
The S in sensual delight
The R in the meaning of romance
The I in I want what you two got!

Stunning Diamonds

I sit in awe as the sun shines brightly around me
A great love alive speaking of divine destiny
The birds are singing when there are none to be found
The chimes are ringing loudly yet making no sound

Two hearts alive following the magical signs
A sweet precious melody that always rhymes
A song of the heart, mind body and soul
A love so strong; it has no choice but to grow

Angel eyes, such a smile it lights up my life
A precious dream come true, there is no strife
First time I laid my eyes upon you I knew
The heavens presented a great love for me and you

You are my rock, my gem, a diamond that shines
What was missing came at exactly the right time
Not one doubt, hesitation, nothing to contemplate
Two hearts singing blissfully of a perfect divine fate

My heart has always been connected to yours
Always knowing it was there for you to adore
Pure love in your eyes, a soul that captures mine
A gift always in place and will be until the end of time

The Angels are singing; around us from the start
Singing sweet praises, that we followed our hearts
They celebrate daily, touching us with their wings
Until that final day when you present me with that ring

Sweet Delectable Sin

Your loins are a hot, massive ball of fire
Moaning, groaning full of raging desire
Touching me with endless volcanic destruction
Taunting and teasing me with your seduction

Juices flowing and delicately being placed
On such a naughty and delectable face
You reach for me starting with my neck
Slowing moving down; this I won't regret

Stopping at my breasts, my nipples you tease
You sure know how to handle these firm babies
Sucking and grasping such sweet ecstasy
My blossom developing quite the roaring sea

Sweet; yet salty skin under your devouring tongue
Turned on like crazy; never wanting this done
Lips craving the taste and smell of the sweet south
You drive me so insane and make me want to shout

Lashing and licking every inch of my body
Not stopping; only wanting to feast and devour
Uttering sassy and naughty words from your lips
All the while grabbing my sleek and curvy hips

Sweetest Song

You are an infinite, delicate, breath taking breeze
Eyes that out do the depth of the deepest seas
Together we spell and create the sweetest destiny
Insurmountable joy and unsurpassable glee

Visions, dreams, an insatiable passionate love
The core of what all fairytale endings are made of
Can't keep my eyes off of you, head spinning around
You stole my heart like a thief in the night, making no sound

I've wasted so much time; now here you are ready to shine
Two hearts joined as one beating perfectly in blissful rhyme
No longer a fantasy or wish; but now a dream come true
I wish to write, embrace and sing the sweetest song for you

There's a dime a dozen, fifty – fifty and one in a million
But baby you got it all and then some, you're one in a zillion
Sweet rapture, heart pulsating wildly out of control
I found you my sweet Angel eyes; I'll never let you go

The Divine Gift

The love we share today shines
From sunrise to sunrise
Growing brighter day to day
As we share our lives

Growing further into one soul
One heart and one mind
As our life together brings new
Meaning to love and oneness

So our love brings new meaning to life
A life anew magnifying into
A perfect dream come true
The miracle of love is that love is given to us

To give to one another, to share in, to care in
Too laugh in, to cry in, to grow in
Thank you for hearing my thoughts, understanding
My dreams and being my best friend

For filling my life with inner music
And loving me without end, for this
Love is a bright smile to share
An ear to listen and a heart to care

All of these things I have in you
Your dedication never falters
Eyes that speak of divine love
Courage that has given me hope
A heart that speaks only truth
Inspiration for my soul to further grow

The Night That Never Ends

The lights are dimmed low; it's just you and me
A gateway of hot love into blissful eternity
Sweat pouring down your shimmering chest
A b c d e f g - baby you've more than passed the test

Delicate silhouettes of your ravenous body in my face
Taking me higher into oblivion; right into outer space
Your beauty baffles me; head to toe and inside out
You drive me straight over the top; just want to shout

Candles burning and smoldering so hot and bright
Climbing the walls; baby you put the meaning into dynamite
Nothing compares to the depths of your fiery, passionate love
A shooting star meteorite; coming down on me from above

You entered the room; I fell apart – the rooms on fire
Running circles in my head, such sweet and sultry desire
Eyes penetrating me, swallowing me whole; won't let me go
Your kiss is the Garden of Eden; such passion you bestow

Drawn to you like bumblebees to honey and white on rice
Rockin' my night and day; you're my definition of paradise
Taking me in further, deeper - shooting right around the bend
A dream come true and love of a lifetime, the night that never ends

The Perfect Match

Once in a lifetime true love comes
It's a precious gift given to the two
It stands the longest test of time
Even when words don't rhyme

The hearts of two cannot deny
What the great divine has created
A love so deep never separated
Torn at heart but never really apart

Souls connected for all an eternity
For a love that was created and meant to be
A love that returns again and once more
Specifically for the two of them to adore

For from the beginning as warm as the sun
The energies alive knowing there is one
Their journey is never over, never done
Destiny states they will always be one

Over and over they divinely fall
It's a true love that conquers all
Love your life don't ever feel blue
This love will come when it is meant too

The Sweetest Sin

I feel heaven, I feel peace
I see all that lies deeply beneath
You touch my heart and my soul
My inner fountain continually grows

Two souls that take a new flight
Destined for love and divine sight
The mind is sleeping; a heart calls
A livened energies embrace and fall

A masculine energy shining so bright
A feminine counterpart of sheer delight
Both courageous, strong and true
Divine gifts deeply embedded in the two

Her love lies in the palm of his hands
He is the brave heart of all the lands
She holds the golden key to his heart
It is due to this; that they will never part

Two souls that had it right from the start
This love is the purest of all hearts
A mysterious sparkle in her eyes
A divine presence he cannot deny

Caught and trapped in your sexy seductive glance
Unfathomly intertwined in your ravenous romance
Thighs quivering in utter sheer delight
Blown into oblivion on a sultry starry night

Body engulfing the fullness of your hands
An ultimate fantasy; fairest of all the lands
Loins a fire – scorching on a hot summer night
Screaming hot ecstasy wildly connected in full flight

There Will Never Be Another

We come to each other in the joy of night
Out of the mind and out of plain sight
Always on perfect time and the perfect place
The sweetest ecstasy our own sacred space

Merging our energies such beauty sown
Every breath taking color of the rainbow
We touch and connect with the deepest part
Joined together in emerald green at the chakra heart

Together we share such a radiant perfect bliss
Sharing the most perfect gift; an orgasmic astral kiss
Two energies dancing with such passionate fire
Burning hot, magnetic rhythm, heartfelt desire

Two pulsating bright burning flames become one
Dynamic energy that far surpasses the brilliant sun
Knowing one another's' thoughts and deepest feelings
Sharing the same vibration and frequency of dreaming

A connection and bond so strong, impossible to deny
An un-canny love representing every star in the sky
Pre-ordained from the beginning; signed and sealed
There is a magnet and there is steel; but this is beyond real

Spiritually and emotionally connected; divinely strong
A choir of Angels around them singing a precious song
One carrying the other like divine footprints in the sand
Like Peter Pan and Tinker Bell off to never never-land

I will now add my own touch to this loving poem
What masterfully perfect love you have always shown
To my deep and passionately steadily burning heart
You my precious love were my desire from the start`

I always thought no man could ever compare to you
Only because you are beyond perfect in all you say and do
But now I know for sure that this is really the spoken truth
Because I have given my whole heart to and married you

They can call this what they will, no one should be keeping score

And there is no need because with you there is much to adore
We have written our words of love and poetic verse for a time
Something we do together in nature and I too now even rhyme

To be the perfect match, both must share the same talents and gifts
And you my beautiful and gorgeous love came to me with just this
You are the ache in my side when I wake up without you there
You are the perfect breeze blowing with such tender loving care

Your love is truly perfect and unmistakably blessed in all that you do
For even the tiniest children and animals have their eyes set on you
To watch you in action and hear the beautiful words from your voice
Makes me fall in love with you all over again, I never had a choice

Wild Butterflies

One look into your breath taking magnetic eyes
Was all it took, crazy, passionate, wild butterflies
You had me from the start, completely stole my heart
Never had a chance, stitch by stitch I came apart

Love at first site came true the moment I laid eyes on you
Didn't believe it at first; now I just want to say I do
It's so unbelievable to be so madly, crazy in love
Cut from the same cloth and delivered from above

That first kiss leaves no words to possibly describe
All the emotions and feelings pouring out from inside
Your precious soul represents the most beautiful rose
An aura so blinding made and paved of streets of gold

There is no other you; made and designed meticulously
Radiant, passionate roaring lion; you're the brave heart for me
Beat all the odds, fought conquered and battled all strife
You are my Angel of the night and the love of my life

You Are the Love of My Life

True love comes to all those who believe
The divine has brought you before me to see
I sit in awe and can't believe my eyes
I knew you were coming but not the time

My heart soars burning a brilliant fire
My feet in mid air, it's you I desire
That smile won't leave my face
So much love you have left in place

You are always on my mind night and day
This feeling of true bliss I want to stay
Butterflies galore can't catch my breath
You touch me with such sweet tenderness

That space in your arms was made for me
The heart that sings speaks of true destiny
Such a miracle and beautiful blessing you are
You light my night; beautiful shooting star

Your kisses capture me, always steal my heart
We knew the gift we are right from the start
That first look, touch, that very first glance
Hook, line and sinker, we never had a chance

You took my breath away and had me from the start
Without saying a word, you reached in and stole my heart
Lost in your eyes, engulfed by your precious soul
Our beautiful garden blossoms, daily it grows

I have waited very patiently for you to come along
It is you who will sing to me the most beautiful song
I feel you night and day, even when you're not here
You have my heart, my all; I will love you year after year

Your Blinding Light

Physically, spiritually and emotionally strong
You and I are right where we belong
A passion far beyond the laws of gravity
One untouchable to man; a deep inner intensity

The ability of two souls to soar and mould creating one
The need to spread our wings when in essence we need none
The beauty of two immaculate souls; joy and peace hovering
The love they once shared, re-opened and rediscovering

A beginning and an end, you and I a true Godsend
Not only shining as one, but two, as the two become one
So much hope to share with the world, a great deal of work to be done
The brightest star in the galaxy made of two
The one and only star designed and made of me and you

My heart and soul spill-eth over, luckier than a four leaf clover
To feel your constant and undying love
To recognize and appreciate a most precious gift
One that could only be sent by heaven above

To know that God has chosen me to be your lady
Putting your precious heart into my hands
For me to care for and treasure; the kindest of all lands
Only to be given back more that I could ever have dreamed of
A love so pure, one purer than the whitest of snow

That ocean pearl deeply buried on the ocean floor
Waiting for what seemed an eternity, for the one she could truly adore
A beauty that could only be uncovered by you
You are the man I love and have always loved
You sincerely are my dream come true

Your Erotic Ways

You had me from hello; before I first laid eyes upon you
You grabbed a hold of my heart and had it in tow
To fight or resist this dynamic, erotic and fiery
Connection would be most impossible I know
Day and night and night and day you make
My garden blossom, flourish and grow

My eyes cannot wander for they are
Permanently blinded by you and only you
You knocked me off of my feet and engrained
Your love into my eyes of sky blue
Your glance pierces through me like
A scorching, electric lightening rod

Burning and cascading, delicately through me
In you and your make up there is not one flaw
You undress me with your come hither eyes
How I love your tantalizing, sexy demise
You melt me time and time again
Straight into orbit my heart is sent

Can't keep my hands off of any of you
Nor do I ever wish or even want to
With you there is never a later or maybe
Take me in repeatedly; I'm all yours baby
The man who had rocked my world once before
Standing before me once again offering his
Erotic, hot fiery insatiable passion to me yet again

You can touch my sacred place from across the room
No camera lens required because you've got the zoom
Those who see us always yell – get a room
What they do know is that our hearts are in full bloom
You make love to me without uttering one single word
Your amazing lips teasing me – not ever missing one curve
I could make a living out of watching you pass on by
Wanting you for now and forever right here by my side

The love we make is like a 7 on the rector scale earthquake
Your dirty, you're passionate, you make my inner thighs shake
I love the way you tease me with just one hot fiery glance

Making mad passionate love together we never stood a chance
I want you day and night and never stop thinking of you
In the bedroom, out in nature, anywhere to bark at the moon
God I want you, desire you, yearn for you all day and night
The wild passionate sexy love you make to me is out of sight

You're Everything

In times of blue when life and your surroundings trouble you
I'm here for you, now and always for you are my dream come true
My love for you reaches the red fiery moon
It's the brightest light on the darkest night

To coddle, comfort and hold you is all I want to do
Pick you up when you're down take the blue from your blue
To be the wind beneath your wings, whisper sweetness in your ear
Fill your heart with bliss, knowing that my heart holds you so dear

I want to be your fiery warmth on a cold winter's night
Be the loving hand that guides you if you ever lose site
The fresh air that you breathe if you're ever in need
The makings of your beautiful garden, your ultimate seed

If you could only see what you truly mean to me
I want to give you my everything, my all
Be there at every waking moment to catch you when you fall
While I can breathe and comprehend, I want to be your everything

Your Sweet, Precious Embrace

You are something else and then some
Never a day goes by when you're not the one
From start, middle to the very end of time
You are the one who makes my life rhyme

Nothing can ever replace your sweet, precious embrace
The way you caress my hair and gently touch my face
Massages that know exactly what to do and where to go
You are the perfect one for me, I always want you to know

How precious you are to me and have always been
You touch my heart so deeply and always make me grin
I adore the man you are today and the man you were before
I would travel the globe to be with you and swim shore to shore

You're My Precious Angel

Your arms are my castle your heart is my sky
Through eternity it has only ever been you and I
Walk through the fragrant garden of my heart
It is there we are connected and shall never ever part

When you look at me I am breathless, down on my knees
Your love I never wished to be cured of; my favorite disease
Ordinary no, I really don't think so not a love this true
The sound of your sexy voice sends me to the moon

You send shivers straight up and down my spine
Glorious seduction; my delicious magnetic wind chime
A touch that renders me paralyzed no words to describe
I love you ever hour of the day; because of you my heart thrives

Your smile made of blinding; divine golden light
Engrained in my heart permanently you never leave my sight
There is truly only one thing that I really wish to do
And that is spending the rest of my days loving you

There isn't anything about you that's not perfect for me
Oh how I love you and only you, as far as the eyes can see
You engulf me day and night with such precious delight
How I adore you my sweet love, you're my perfect knight